GUIDE TO RECOVERY FROM COMPLEX PTSD

Overcoming Childhood Trauma, Toxic and Unhealthy Relationships, Emotional Abuse, Gaslighting and Narcissistic Abuse

LINDA WALKER

INTRODUCTION

I grew up in a world colored by shadows, a life dominated by the echoes of a painful past. It wasn't until much later in life that I would come to understand the true weight of those early years. This journey, chronicled in the following pages, is one of resilience, transformation, and ultimately, triumph over the insidious grasp of Complex PTSD.

As I look back, I see a child, wide-eyed and hopeful, navigating a world fraught with landmines of trauma. The memories are fragmented, like shattered glass, each piece holding a fragment of pain that I would carry for years. Back then, I lacked the vocabulary to describe the heaviness that settled within my chest, the unease that became my constant companion.

It was in the dance of relationships that the patterns emerged. Each connection seemed to carry with it a familiar toxicity, a subtle echo of the past. At first, I couldn't discern the source of the unease, the gnawing feeling that something was fundamentally askew. It was as if I was trapped in a maze, unable to find my way out.

The turning point came when I stumbled upon the concept of Complex PTSD. The words resonated with a clarity that sent shivers down my spine. Suddenly, the pieces began to align, the puzzle of my life taking shape before my eyes. This wasn't just about isolated incidents, but a life from years of silent suffering.

With newfound understanding came the first fragile steps towards healing. It was a step that demanded courage, a willingness to confront the ghosts of the past and a commitment to forge a different path forward. Therapy became my sanctuary, a space where I could unravel the tangled threads of my history, guided by a compassionate hand.

In the process, I learned to peel back the layers of self-blame and shame, recognizing that the scars I carried were not a reflection of my worth. They were battle wounds, evidence of a spirit that had endured and survived. It was a revelation that sparked a slow but steady transformation.

One of the most formidable challenges lay in dismantling the web of unhealthy relationships that had woven themselves into my life. It required a seismic shift in perspective, a reclamation of agency that had long been dormant. Setting boundaries became an act of self-preservation, a declaration of my inherent value.

Identifying emotional abuse and gaslighting was like pulling back a curtain to reveal the mechanics of manipulation. It was a painful reckoning, but also a moment of profound empowerment. No longer was I captive to the whims of others' distortions. I stood firm in my truth, refusing to allow it to be distorted or silenced.

The journey through recovery from narcissistic abuse was perhaps the most arduous of all. It meant confronting the shadows of my own self-worth, untangling the insidious beliefs that had taken root. Slowly, I learned to recognize the strength that had always resided within me, a flame that could not be extinguished by the darkness.

Therapeutic approaches became my toolkit, each session a step towards reclaiming my sense of self. EMDR unlocked doors I didn't even know were there, releasing the grip of buried memories. Cognitive Behavioral Therapy provided a roadmap for rewiring thought patterns, offering a path to healthier relationships, both with myself and others.

Yet, it wasn't just the clinical approaches that guided me. Mindfulness and self-compassion became touchstones in my daily life, reminding me to be present in each moment, to extend the same kindness to myself that I so readily offered to others. They were anchors in the storm, grounding me in a sense of worthiness that no external validation could provide.

Through it all, self-care emerged as both armor and balm. It meant prioritizing my physical, emotional, and mental well-being, recognizing that I was worthy of that investment. Building resilience became an ongoing practice, a commitment to face each day with an open heart, even in the face of triggers and flashbacks.

Today, as I stand on the other side of transformation, I am not defined by the scars of my past, but by the strength it took to heal. The echoes of childhood trauma have quieted, replaced by the steady rhythm of my own heartbeat, a reminder that I am here, I am whole, and I am enough.

This book is an offering born from that journey, a guide for those who walk a similar path. It is a testament to the possibility of healing, a roadmap for those who may feel lost in their own pain.

CONTENTS

- Focusing on Self-Care: Physical, Emotional, and Mental Well-being
- Building Resilience: Strategies for Coping with Triggers and Flashbacks
- Establishing Supportive Connections: Finding Your Community
- Tapping into Your Inner Strength: Empowerment and Growth

CHAPTER 8: EMBRACING CHANGE AND THRIVING BEYOND TRAUMA

- Embracing the Healing Journey: A Lifelong Process
- Acknowledging Milestones: Recognizing Progress
- Cultivating a Purposeful and Gratifying Life
- Extending Support to Others on Their Healing Journey

CHAPTER 1

THE COMPLEXITY OF PTSD

Defining Complex Post-Traumatic Stress Disorder

In the quiet sanctum of a therapist's office, I encountered a term that would become the cornerstone of my journey: Complex Post-Traumatic Stress Disorder, or Complex PTSD. Those words resonated with a depth that eluded immediate comprehension, but I sensed their gravity.

Complex PTSD, I would come to learn, transcends a solitary wound, evolving into a constellation of scars etched upon the soul. It emerges from extended exposure to traumatic events, often entangled within interpersonal relationships, where trust and security were shattered. Unlike its more familiar counterpart, PTSD, which typically arises from discrete incidents, Complex PTSD weaves a narrative from enduring pain.

This nuanced form of trauma permeates life in multifaceted ways; it's the restless nights haunted by vivid recollections, the ever-watchful eye that transforms every corner into a potential threat, the capricious waves of emotion that threaten to overwhelm reason.

Defining Complex PTSD encompasses acknowledging its profound influence on the psyche, physique, and essence of an individual. It is an injury that transcends the surface, a fracture in the very bedrock of one's identity. It reaches into the core of our existence, reshaping how we perceive ourselves, others, and the world at large.

As I delved deeper into this definition, I found solace in understanding that I was not isolated in this struggle. It provided a framework, a lexicon to articulate the tempest within. It enabled me to validate my experiences, to recognize that the turmoil I felt was not indicative of frailty, but rather a testament to the fortitude it took to endure.

Comprehending Complex PTSD is not a mere intellectual exercise; it is a feat of reclaiming dominion over one's narrative. It is a proclamation that one's pain bears a name, and that name holds sway. It is a pivotal initial stride on the road to recovery, a beacon in the obscurity, illuminating the path ahead.

Differentiating Complex PTSD from Other Trauma Types

As I delved further to understanding Complex PTSD, it became apparent that this form of trauma held distinct characteristics setting it apart from its better-known counterpart, PTSD. It was crucial to grasp these nuances, for it laid the foundation for tailored healing and recovery.

While PTSD often emerges from singular, isolated incidents of trauma, Complex PTSD takes root in prolonged exposure to distressing situations, frequently within the context of interpersonal relationships. It's a crucial distinction, one that alters recovery. For me, recognizing this difference was akin to deciphering a complex code; it held the keys to unlocking a more precise path toward healing.

Complex PTSD carries with it a unique set of symptoms, weaving complex emotional, psychological, and physical responses. The flashbacks and nightmares, hallmarks of PTSD, are joined by a constellation of other manifestations. These may include pervasive feelings of shame and guilt, difficulty forming and maintaining relationships, and a persistent sense of emptiness or detachment.

One of the defining features of Complex PTSD is the impact it has on self-identity. Unlike PTSD, where the sense of self may remain relatively intact, Complex PTSD often fractures the core of one's identity. It's as though the very foundation upon which we build our understanding of who we are has been shaken. This fundamental shift requires a different approach to healing, one that addresses the profound existential questions that arise.

Differentiating between these two forms of trauma is not about diminishing the significance of either. Rather, it's about recognizing that each demands a tailored approach to recovery. It's akin to acknowledging that while two trees may share the same forest, their roots and branches are unique, and thus require distinct care and nurturing.

In my own journey, this understanding was a revelation. It allowed me to shed the expectation that my healing should follow a prescribed path. It gave me permission to honor the complexity of my experience and embrace a recovery journey that was as individual as I was.

As we navigate this terrain together, it's important to hold space for this distinction. It provides a roadmap, a compass by which to navigate the sometimes bewildering landscape of recovery. It reminds us that healing is a deeply personal journey guided by the contours of our own unique experiences.

How Childhood Trauma Impacts Adult Well-being

The echoes of childhood are not confined to the past; they reverberate through the chambers of our adult lives, shaping the very essence of our well-being. Understanding the profound impact of childhood trauma is similar to peering through a window into the genesis of our struggles and triumphs.

For those of us who carry the weight of Complex PTSD, childhood was often a battleground, a terrain fraught with landmines of emotional and psychological upheaval. It was a time when the world was meant to be a sanctuary, a cocoon of safety and nurturance. Yet, for many, it was a crucible of uncertainty and fear.

Childhood trauma can manifest in a multitude of forms. It may be the overt brutality of physical or sexual abuse, leaving scars that linger long into adulthood. It may be the insidious erosion of emotional neglect, a silent void that gnaws at the edges of one's sense of self-worth. It may be the steady drip of verbal aggression, each word a drop in the torrent that wears away at the bedrock of one's confidence.

These early experiences imprint themselves upon the psyche, shaping the lens through which we view ourselves and the world around us. They become the foundation upon which we build our sense of self, influencing our beliefs about our worthiness, our capacity for love, and our ability to trust.

For those of us navigating Complex PTSD, this impact is profound. It's a wound that often remains hidden, masked by the veneer of adulthood. Yet, its tendrils reach into every facet of our lives, coloring our relationships, our self-perception, and our capacity to experience joy and connection.

Understanding the link between childhood trauma and adult well-being is not an exercise in blame or victimhood; it is an act of profound compassion. It's an acknowledgment that the wounds of the past continue to shape our present, and that by shining a light on them, we can begin the process of healing.

In my own journey, this revelation was a seismic shift. It allowed me to hold my inner child with tenderness and care, recognizing that the pain she endured had left an indelible mark. It gave me permission to grieve for the innocence that was stolen, and to embark on a journey of reclaiming my sense of self.

As we navigate this terrain together, it's important to do so with gentleness and self-compassion. It's a recognition that the scars of childhood trauma are not a reflection of our worth, but a testament to our resilience. They are the roadmap to our healing, guiding us towards a future where we can rewrite the narrative of our lives.

Recognizing Patterns of Harmful Relationships and Abuse

In our lives, relationships weave the narrative of our existence. They hold the power to uplift, to nurture, and to inspire. Yet, for those of us touched by Complex PTSD, relationships can also be the crucible of our deepest wounds.

Recognizing the patterns of harmful relationships and abuse is an essential facet of understanding the complexities of our journey. It requires a willingness to turn a discerning eye towards the dynamics that have shaped our interactions with others, often from a young age.

For many of us, the seeds of these patterns were sown in the soil of childhood. It was within the crucible of family dynamics that we first learned what it meant to love, to trust, and to be valued. Yet, for some, it was also a terrain marked by betrayal, by neglect, or by outright cruelty.

These early experiences can set the stage for a lifetime of relational dynamics that mirror the patterns of our past. It may manifest in a tendency to attract partners who mirror the behaviors of our caretakers, perpetuating cycles of abuse. It may be a pattern of subsuming our own needs in order to maintain a sense of connection, at the expense of our own well-being.

Recognizing these patterns is not an indictment of our worth or our capacity to love; it is an act of reclaiming agency over the narrative of our relationships. It's an acknowledgment that the dynamics we learned in childhood are not our destiny, but rather a starting point from which we can evolve and grow.

This recognition was a watershed moment. It allowed me to see the threads that wove through my own relational history, illuminating the ways in which I had unwittingly perpetuated cycles of harm. It gave me the power to pause, to reflect, and to choose a different path forward.

Understanding these patterns also empowers us to set boundaries, a crucial aspect of navigating healthy relationships. It means recognizing that we have the right to define our own worth and to expect that worth to be honored by those with whom we share our lives.

CHAPTER 2

EARLY LIFE TRAUMA

Tracing the Origin: Exploring Early Experiences

In the hushed corners of memory, fragments of my early years lay dormant, waiting to be acknowledged. It was a delicate excavation, each recollection a brushstroke on the canvas of my past. As I delved into those formative moments, I unearthed joy and sorrow, love and neglect.

The scent of my grandmother's kitchen, warm and inviting, wove a comforting cocoon around my childhood. Her laughter was the soundtrack of those tender years, a melody that danced through the rooms of her cozy home. There, amidst the clatter of pots and pans, I found solace in the simple act of baking cookies, a ritual that transcended generations.

Yet, even within cherished moments, there were shadows. Whispers of arguments carried on the wind, the tension that hung heavy in the air. It was a dissonance I couldn't quite grasp at the time, a disquiet that settled in the spaces between laughter and shared secrets.

As I grew, so did my awareness of the world beyond our haven. The playground became a stage where the intricacies of human interaction unfurled. It was a place of alliances and rivalries, a microcosm of the complex dynamics that would come to shape my understanding of relationships.

The sting of rejection, sharp and unfamiliar, etched its mark on my tender heart. It was a rite of passage that left me vulnerable, questioning my worthiness of connection. Those early bruises, though invisible to the eye, would leave their imprint, influencing the way I navigated relationships in years to come.

In adolescence, my world shifted once more. The halls of high school were a tapestry of cliques and insecurities, a battlefield where fragile egos vied for validation. It was here that I first encountered the insidious tendrils of emotional manipulation, the subtle art of wielding words as weapons.

I watched as friendships unraveled, threads of trust fraying under the weight of betrayal. The wounds inflicted were not always visible, but their impact was no less profound. It was a classroom in resilience, a crash course in discerning the difference between genuine connection and hollow facades.

With the passing of time, the contours of my early experiences began to sharpen into focus. The seeds of Complex PTSD had been sown in the soil of my youth, their roots entwining with the narrative of my upbringing. It was a revelation that both unsettled and empowered me, for in understanding the source, I found the key to unravelling its hold.

As I stand on the threshold of this journey, I carry with me the knowledge that the past is not a stagnant canvas, but a living tapestry that weaves its influence into the present. In tracing the origin of my early experiences, I aspire on a path of healing, guided by the understanding that acknowledging the wounds of the past is the first step towards reclaiming the narrative of my future.

How Childhood Trauma Manifests in Adulthood

The echoes of my childhood reverberate through the chambers of my adult life, their resonance both subtle and profound. It is in the patterns of behavior, the intricacies of relationships, that the fingerprints of early trauma leave their indelible mark.

In intimacy, I found myself stumbling over the shards of my past. Walls constructed in self-preservation became barriers to connection, guarding a heart scarred by the wounds of yesteryears. The vulnerability required to trust and be trusted felt like navigating treacherous terrain, a testament to the enduring legacy of childhood wounds.

The specter of abandonment cast its long shadow, a specter that haunted my relationships like a ghost in the night. The fear of being left behind, of not being enough, became a silent companion in moments of vulnerability. It was a narrative that whispered in the quiet spaces, a refrain that echoed through the chambers of my heart.

Yet, it wasn't only in matters of the heart that the tendrils of childhood trauma made their presence known. They manifested in the way I navigated the world, the choices I made, the boundaries I struggled to set. The patterns of coping forged in the crucible of early adversity shaped the lens through which I viewed myself and others.

As I moved through adulthood, I began to recognize the ways in which these patterns played out. The tendency to overextend myself, to put the needs of others before my own, was a reflection of a belief system rooted in self-sacrifice. The reluctance to ask for help, a vestige of a time when vulnerability was met with indifference or rejection.

In the part of work and achievement, the drive to excel became a double-edged sword. It was a pursuit born of a hunger for validation, a longing to prove my worthiness in a world that had once made me question it. The pursuit of success, while admirable in its ambition, carried with it the weight of unmet childhood needs.

Yet, woven these challenges was a thread of resilience. It was the same resilience that had carried me through the storms of my early years, a force that refused to be extinguished. It was the resilience that propelled me forward, urging me to confront the patterns that no longer served me, to rewrite the narrative of my adulthood.

In this journey, I have come to understand that acknowledging the ways in which childhood trauma manifests in adulthood is not an indictment, but an invitation. It is an invitation to compassion, to self-reflection, to the profound act of reclaiming agency over my own narrative.

As I stand at the intersection of past and present, I do so with the knowledge that I am not defined by the scars of my history, but by the strength it took to heal. With each step forward, I carry with me the wisdom gleaned from the echoes of my childhood, a compass that guides me towards a future of possibility, resilience, and boundless potential.

Breaking Generational Patterns of Hurt

In the stillness of self-reflection, I confront a truth both daunting and liberating: the patterns of hurt are not confined to my own story, but are threads woven into generations past. It is a revelation that carries with it a weighty responsibility, but also the promise of profound transformation.

As I trace the lineage of my family, I see the familiar contours of pain etched into the narrative. The unspoken wounds, the secrets held close, the legacy of unhealed traumas passed down like an heirloom. It is a legacy that stretches back through the annals of time, a silent witness to the resilience and survival of those who came before me.

Yet, in acknowledging this inheritance of hurt, I find within it the seeds of possibility. For if pain can be passed down through generations, so too can healing. It is a truth that sparks a spark of hope, a belief in the power of transformation that transcends time and lineage.

The journey to break generational patterns of hurt begins with the courageous act of bearing witness to the pain that has been passed down. It requires a willingness to confront the shadows of the past, to sit with the discomfort, and to hold space for the stories that have long been silenced.

In this process, I find allies in the stories of those who came before me. Their resilience becomes a beacon, a testament to the human capacity for survival and growth. It is a reminder that the legacy of pain does not define us, but rather serves as a backdrop against which our own journey of healing unfolds.

Breaking generational patterns of hurt is a complex and nuanced endeavor. It requires a commitment to self-awareness, a willingness to challenge ingrained beliefs and behaviors. It is a process of unlearning and relearning, of untangling the threads of inherited pain and weaving a new narrative of resilience and healing.

As I go on this transformative journey, I am acutely aware of the impact it carries beyond my own story. It is a ripple effect that extends far beyond the confines of my own experience, touching the lives of those who will come after me. It is a legacy of healing, a testament to the power of one individual's willingness to confront the ghosts of the past.

In this act of breaking generational patterns of hurt, I step into the role of a torchbearer, carrying the flame of healing forward. It is a responsibility I bear with both humility and determination, knowing that each step I take towards my own healing is a step towards liberation for those who will follow.

As I stand at the intersection of past and future, I do so with a profound sense of purpose. In breaking the chains of generational pain, I not only free myself, but pave the way for a legacy of resilience and healing that will echo through the corridors of time. It is a legacy that transcends bloodlines, a testament to the enduring power of the human spirit.

Tools for Coping and Processing Childhood Trauma

In the crucible of healing, I have come to understand that the journey is not a solitary one. It is a collaborative effort between past and present, a dance between the wounded child within and the resilient adult I have become. In this sacred space of transformation, I have gathered a toolkit of strategies to navigate childhood trauma.

At the heart of this toolkit lies the power of self-compassion. It is the gentle embrace I offer to the wounded parts of myself, a balm for the hurts that still echo in the chambers of my heart. It is a reminder that I am worthy of kindness, of tenderness, of the same love I so readily extend to others.

Therapy has become a cornerstone of my healing journey, a sanctuary where I can unfurl the layers of my story in the presence of a compassionate witness. It is a space where the fragments of memory find coherence, where my narrative are woven into understanding. Through the guidance of a skilled therapist, I have unearthed buried truths, navigated the labyrinth of emotions, and forged a path towards wholeness.

Mindfulness has emerged as a steadfast companion on this journey. It is the practice of being present in each moment, of grounding myself in the here and now. Through mindful awareness, I have learned to witness my thoughts and emotions without judgment, to cultivate a sense of inner stillness amidst the storm.

Journaling has become an anchor, a vessel to hold the weight of my thoughts and feelings. It is within the pages of my journal that I find refuge, a space where I can speak my truth without reservation. Through the act of writing, I release the pent-up emotions, untangle the threads of confusion, and find clarity amidst the chaos.

The practice of somatic healing has been a revelation, a bridge between the language of the body and the language of the soul. Through gentle movement and mindful breath, I have learned to listen to the whispers of my body, to honor its wisdom, and to release the stored tension that bears witness to the traumas of the past.

As I go through coping and processing childhood trauma, I am acutely aware of the importance of self-care. It is a commitment to nurturing my physical, emotional, and mental well-being, a recognition that I am deserving of the same care and attention I so readily offer to others. Whether through nourishing meals, restful sleep, or moments of quiet reflection, self-care is a cornerstone of my healing practice.

Above all, I have come to understand that the journey of healing is not linear, but that of progress and setbacks, of moments of clarity and moments of uncertainty. It is a testament to the resilience of the human spirit, a reminder that even in the face of immense pain, there is the potential for profound transformation.

As I stand at the threshold of this chapter, I do so with a sense of gratitude for the tools that have illuminated my path. They are the lanterns that guide me through the darkness, the compass that points towards a future of possibility and wholeness. In the embrace of these tools, I find the strength to continue this sacred journey of healing.

CHAPTER 3

NAVIGATING UNHEALTHY RELATIONSHIPS

Recognizing Toxic Relationship Dynamics

For human connections, toxicity often hides in plain sight, masked by smiles and kind gestures. It's a subtle undertow, where warning signs can be easily dismissed or overlooked. I, too, have traversed this treacherous terrain, blinded by hope and the belief in the innate goodness of those around me.

Toxic relationship dynamics manifest in myriad ways. It might be the friend who consistently undermines your achievements, or the partner whose love seems conditional on compliance. It's the family member whose words cut deeper than any blade, or the coworker who thrives on sowing discord. What unites them is their capacity to erode your sense of self, the slow erosion of your boundaries until they are but a distant memory.

Spotting these dynamics requires a shift in perception, a readiness to peer beneath the surface interactions. It demands a courageous examination of the power dynamics at play, an acknowledgment that not all relationships are constructed on a foundation of mutual respect and support.

For me, this awakening unfolded gradually. It commenced with a persistent unease, a nagging feeling that something was fundamentally awry. It was in the subtle moments—the veiled barbs, the dismissive glances—that left me questioning my own worth. It was the pattern of feeling depleted after interactions, a heaviness settling in my chest.

As I delved deeper, I unearthed the recurring themes that defined these relationships. The skewed power dynamics, the absence of reciprocity, the emotional manipulation—all became glaringly evident. It was as though a veil had been lifted, revealing a landscape I had been navigating blindly.

Identifying toxic dynamics is no small feat. It necessitates trusting your instincts, validating the discomfort that arises. It means daring to question the established norms, to challenge the narratives that may have become ingrained over time. It is a courageous act of reclaiming agency, of affirming, "I deserve better."

In the journey of recovery, this recognition forms the bedrock of transformation. It is the pivotal moment when you seize the reins of your own narrative, when you refuse to be complicit in a dynamic that dims your light. It is a declaration of self-worth, a resounding affirmation that you are deserving of relationships that nurture, uplift, and honor the essence of who you are.

Remember, you are not alone in this. Seek support, lean on those who can offer perspective and validation. Together, we untangle the threads of toxic dynamics, weaving a tapestry of relationships that empower and elevate. By recognizing the toxicity, you take the first courageous step toward a future defined by healthy, nourishing connections.

Understanding Codependency and Enabling Behaviors

For relationships, codependency often lurks, silently but tenaciously. It's a subtle dynamic, one where boundaries blur, and self-worth becomes entangled with the well-being of another. I know this well, for I too have grappled with the complexities of codependency.

Codependency is a dance of enmeshment, where one's sense of self is enfolded within the needs and desires of another. It's the belief that one's worth is contingent on their ability to meet the demands of a relationship, often at the expense of their own well-being. It's a pattern of putting others' needs before one's own, driven by a deep-seated fear of abandonment or rejection.

For me, the seeds of codependency were sown in the soil of early relationships. The belief that my value lay in being the caretaker, the fixer, took root. It was a role that offered a semblance of control, a way to navigate the unpredictable of relationships. Yet, it also came at a steep cost—a gradual erosion of my own identity, a diminishing of my own needs and desires.

Understanding codependency means peeling back the layers of conditioning, unraveling the beliefs that had become woven into one's own being. It means confronting the fear of asserting one's own boundaries, of acknowledging that your needs are valid and deserving of acknowledgment.

Breaking free from codependency was a journey of reclamation. It was a process of rediscovering my own autonomy, of recognizing that my worth was not contingent on my ability to meet the needs of others. It meant learning to prioritize self-care, to honor my own desires, and to trust that my well-being was a worthy pursuit in and of itself.

Enabling behaviors, another facet of this, often accompany codependency. It's the compulsion to rescue, to shield others from the consequences of their actions, driven by a desire to maintain the status quo. It's a pattern that stems from a well-intentioned but ultimately misguided belief that by shouldering the burden, we can protect our loved ones from pain.

I too grappled with this compulsion to enable, to smooth over rough edges, to shield others from discomfort. It was a role that seemed noble, selfless even. Yet, over time, I came to see the harm it wrought—not only to myself but to those I sought to protect. It became clear that true growth and healing could only occur when individuals were allowed to confront the consequences of their choices.

Recognizing codependency and enabling behaviors is an act of profound self-compassion. It requires acknowledging the patterns that no longer serve our well-being and summoning the courage to forge a different path. It means learning to hold space for our own needs and desires, even in the face of discomfort or resistance.

As you navigate this terrain, know that you are not alone. Many have walked this path before you, and many will walk it after. Seek support, lean on those who can offer guidance and understanding. Together, we unravel the threads of codependency, weaving a tapestry of relationships rooted in authenticity, mutual respect, and genuine care. By understanding these dynamics, you pave the way for relationships that are built on a foundation of healthy interdependence, where each individual is honored in their unique worth.

Establishing Boundaries and Voicing Your Needs

Boundaries, though invisible, are the scaffolding that support healthy relationships. They are the lines we draw to safeguard our well-being, the space we create to honor our own needs and desires. Learning to establish and uphold boundaries is a cornerstone of navigating healthy relationships, and it's a lesson I learned through trial and error.

For much of my life, the concept of boundaries felt foreign, even daunting. It seemed counterintuitive, a potential source of conflict or rejection. Instead, I defaulted to a pattern of accommodating, of prioritizing others' comfort over my own. It was a strategy aimed at maintaining harmony, but it came at a steep cost—a gradual erosion of my own sense of agency.

Recognizing the need for boundaries is the first step. It means acknowledging that your needs and desires are valid, that you are deserving of respect and consideration. It requires a shift in perspective, a willingness to see boundaries not as barriers, but as bridges to healthier, more authentic connections.

Establishing boundaries is an act of self-love. It's a declaration that your well-being matters, that your feelings and limits are worthy of acknowledgment. It means learning to say "no" without guilt, to voice your needs without fear of reprisal. It's about reclaiming agency over your own life, about shaping your relationships in a way that honors the essence of who you are.

However, setting boundaries is not always met with open arms. It can be met with resistance, with pushback from those accustomed to a different dynamic. This is where the true test of your commitment to self-care lies. It requires standing firm, holding fast to the knowledge that honoring your boundaries is an act of integrity, not a rejection of others.

Voicing your needs is the natural companion to establishing boundaries. It's the articulation of your desires, the expression of your feelings, the affirmation of your own agency. It's a skill that requires practice and patience, especially for those of us who have been conditioned to prioritize others' needs over our own.

For me, finding my voice was a journey of self-discovery. It meant unlearning the belief that my worth was contingent on my ability to please and accommodate. It meant daring to speak up, even when my voice trembled, even when it felt uncomfortable. It was a reclaiming of my own narrative, a declaration that I was worthy of being heard.

Remember, this is a process—a journey of growth and self-discovery. It's about finding the balance between honoring your own needs and respecting the needs of others. It's about recognizing that healthy relationships are built on a foundation of mutual respect and consideration.

As you embark on this path of establishing boundaries and voicing your needs, be gentle with yourself. It's a practice, not a perfection. Seek support from those who understand and validate your journey. Together, we learn to navigate relationships, creating spaces where authenticity, respect, and genuine care flourish. By establishing boundaries and voicing your needs, you cultivate relationships that are grounded in mutual understanding and a deep honoring of each individual's autonomy.

Strategies for Building and Sustaining Healthy Relationships

Building and sustaining healthy relationships is a tapestry woven with intention, communication, and mutual respect. It's a journey that requires active engagement, a commitment to nurturing connections that uplift and empower. Through my own experiences, I've come to understand that healthy relationships are not simply stumbled upon; they are intentionally crafted.

The foundation of a healthy relationship lies in open, honest communication. It's the willingness to share your thoughts, feelings, and needs, and to truly listen to those of your partner. Communication is not merely the exchange of words, but the bridge that connects two hearts, allowing understanding and empathy to flow freely.

For much of my life, I shied away from vulnerability, viewing it as a potential gateway to pain or rejection. I kept my truest self guarded, fearing that exposing my inner world would make me too susceptible to hurt. However, I came to learn that true intimacy is born from vulnerability. It's the willingness to show up as you are, to trust that your authentic self is not only worthy of love but is the very essence of what makes you lovable.

In healthy relationships, there is an equitable balance of give and take. It's an understanding that both parties have needs, desires, and boundaries that deserve acknowledgment. It means recognizing that each individual brings their own unique gifts to the partnership, and that those gifts should be honored and celebrated.

Respect is the cornerstone of any healthy connection. It's the acknowledgment that each person is an autonomous being, deserving of dignity and consideration. It's the commitment to honoring boundaries and making choices that uplift rather than diminish. Respect forms the bedrock of trust, creating a safe space where both individuals can fully be themselves.

Mutual growth and support are the lifeblood of a thriving relationship. It's the recognition that each person is on their own journey of self-discovery and evolution. It's the willingness to stand by one another, offering encouragement, and celebrating milestones. It's about creating a space where both individuals can flourish, both individually and together.

I've also come to understand that healthy relationships require ongoing care and attention. They are not static entities but living, breathing organisms that require nourishment. This means showing up consistently, even when it's challenging. It means being present, being attuned to the needs of your partner, and being willing to adapt and grow together.

Remember, building and sustaining healthy relationships is a practice, not a destination. It's about showing up with intention, with a willingness to learn and grow. It's about recognizing that true connection requires effort, but the rewards are immeasurable.

CHAPTER 4

IDENTIFYING EMOTIONAL ABUSE AND GASLIGHTING

Defining Emotional Abuse and Gaslighting

In human relationships, there exists something darker, merged with manipulation and control. This stuff goes by many names, but its essence remains the same: emotional abuse and gaslighting. To embark on the path of recovery, one must first learn to recognize these insidious forces.

Emotional abuse, a silent predator in relationships, is a complex dance of power and control. It does not announce its presence with thunderous roars, but rather, it slips in like a whisper, insidiously weaving Itself into daily interactions. It is the relentless erosion of self-worth through belittling words, the weight of constant criticism, and the suffocating grip of control. It leaves behind scars that may not be visible to the naked eye but run deep within the psyche.

Gaslighting, its sinister counterpart, is a psychological battleground where reality itself becomes the prize. It is the art of making one question their own perception, sowing seeds of confusion and self-doubt. The gaslighter wields their manipulative prowess with precision, leaving their target adrift in a sea of uncertainty, clinging desperately to the fragments of their own truth. It is a dance of distortion and denial, a carefully choreographed symphony of half-truths and misdirection.

Understanding the intricacies of emotional abuse and gaslighting is similar to turning on a light in a room that has long been shrouded in darkness. It is a revelation that empowers, providing the clarity needed to reclaim one's sense of self. Armed with this knowledge, we embark on the journey of unraveling the web of manipulation and reclaiming our truth.

To define emotional abuse and gaslighting is to dissect the anatomy of toxicity, to peer into the shadows and name the demons that lurk within. It is a process of demystification, of dispelling the illusion that these forces are beyond our comprehension. They are not nebulous specters; they are tangible, recognizable patterns that we have the power to identify and confront.

Emotional abuse, at its core, is an imbalance of power. It thrives on the degradation of self-worth, on the systematic dismantling of confidence. It wears many masks - the cutting words, the demeaning gestures, the relentless criticism. Yet, its essence remains constant: the exertion of dominance through psychological manipulation. It is the partner who belittles every accomplishment, the parent who withholds affection as a means of control, the friend who feeds off the insecurities of others.

Gaslighting, in its insidious elegance, preys on the very foundations of reality. It is the calculated campaign to distort truth, to rewrite history, to make the victim doubt their own senses. It is the subtle undermining, the strategic misdirection, the artful playacting designed to leave the victim questioning their sanity. It is the slow chipping away of confidence, the erosion of trust in one's own perception.

As we delve into the heart of this darkness, we do so not as passive observers, but as warriors armed with knowledge. We are reclaiming the narrative, refusing to be held captive by the tactics of manipulation. In understanding emotional abuse and gaslighting, we are shining a light on the shadows, dispelling the power of these insidious forces.

In the pages that follow, we will dissect these patterns further, equipping ourselves with the tools to recognize and resist. We will reclaim our agency, inch by inch, until we stand firmly in our truth. For it is through understanding that we find the strength to break free, to reclaim our sense of self, and to forge a path towards healing.

Exposing Manipulative Tactics and Psychological Games

To identify emotional abuse and gaslighting is to become intimately acquainted with the tactics employed by those who seek to wield power through manipulation. It is a journey into the heart of darkness, where we confront the subtle yet devastating methods used to control and demean.

Gaslighters are masters of distortion, architects of a reality that serves their own agenda. They operate with a precision that is both chilling and calculated. One of their favored tools is the art of trivialization. In their hands, genuine concerns become exaggerated, blown out of proportion, reduced to mere trifles. The pain, the hurt, the very essence of our experience is minimized, leaving us to question the validity of our emotions.

Deflection is another arrow in the gaslighter's quiver. When confronted with their behavior, they are skilled in the art of redirection, shifting the focus away from their actions and onto the perceived flaws of their victim. It is a subtle yet potent form of manipulation, one that leaves the victim grappling with a sense of unwarranted guilt and self-doubt.

Perhaps the most insidious tactic in the gaslighter's arsenal is outright denial. They are adept at rewriting history, erasing events from the collective memory with a chilling confidence. It is a form of psychological warfare, a calculated attempt to make the victim doubt reality. In the face of such brazen denial, it is easy to feel as though we are adrift in a sea of uncertainty, clinging desperately to the fragments of our own truth.

Emotional abusers, too, have their own arsenal of tactics, each one designed to maintain their grip on power. Humiliation is a favored weapon, a means of asserting dominance through the degradation of the victim. It is the cutting remark, the derisive laughter, the deliberate act of diminishing one's sense of self-worth. It leaves scars that run deep, wounds that may not be visible to the outside world but sear within.

Intimidation is another tool in the emotional abuser's toolkit. It is the subtle threat, the unspoken promise of retribution should the victim dare to assert themselves. It is the pervasive sense of walking on eggshells, of existing in a state of perpetual apprehension. This atmosphere of fear becomes the breeding ground for control, the fertile soil in which manipulation takes root.

Isolation, perhaps one of the most devastating tactics, serves to sever the victim from their support network. The emotional abuser carefully crafts a narrative that paints them as the sole source of solace and understanding. They chip away at the bonds that connect the victim to friends and family, leaving them isolated and vulnerable. It is a calculated strategy, one that ensures the victim's dependence on the abuser for validation and belonging.

Recognizing these tactics is a declaration that we will no longer be held captive by the whims of manipulation. With each unveiled tactic, we reclaim a piece of our agency, fortifying our resolve to break free from the chains that bind us.

In the crucible of understanding, we forge a shield against the manipulation that seeks to control us. We stand tall, armed with the knowledge of these tactics, and we declare that we will not be silenced. Through this newfound clarity, we pave the way for our own healing, reclaiming our narrative and forging a future free from the shadows of manipulation.

Reclaiming Your Reality: Validation and Self-Trust

In the wake of recognizing emotional abuse and gaslighting, a crucial step on the path to recovery is reclaiming our sense of reality. It is a journey of validation, a process of anchoring ourselves in the truth of our experiences, and rebuilding the trust in our own perception.

Validation is the balm that soothes the wounds inflicted by manipulation. It is the acknowledgement that our feelings, our experiences, are valid and worthy of recognition. Too often, victims of emotional abuse and gaslighting find themselves questioning the legitimacy of their emotions, second-guessing the very core of their being. In seeking validation, we turn to those who offer empathy and understanding, who bear witness to our pain without judgment.

Yet, validation must also come from within. It is a process of learning to trust our own intuition, to recognize that our feelings are a compass guiding us through the labyrinth of our experiences. It requires a willingness to silence the cacophony of doubt and listen to the quiet whisper of our inner knowing. It is a journey of self-discovery, of recognizing that our reality is not defined by the perceptions of others, but by the truth that resides within us.

Reclaiming our reality is an act of defiance against the forces that seek to distort it. It is a declaration that we will no longer allow our truth to be eroded by the tactics of manipulation. It is a stance of unwavering self-respect, a commitment to honor the validity of our experiences.

In this journey, we may encounter resistance, both from within ourselves and from external sources. The seeds of doubt planted by years of gaslighting may still linger, their tendrils reaching out in moments of vulnerability. It is important to approach ourselves with gentleness and compassion, to recognize that healing is a process, and that it is okay to falter along the way.

Building self-trust is akin to forging a bridge between our past and our present, between the wounded soul and the resilient spirit. It is a practice that requires patience and persistence, a commitment to nurturing the seed of self-worth that lies within us. Through small acts of self-affirmation, through the cultivation of self-compassion, we fortify this bridge, allowing it to bear the weight of our truth.

To reclaim our reality, we do so with a fierce determination. We recognize that our truth is not contingent on the validation of others, but on the unwavering belief in our own experiences. We stand firm in the knowledge that we are not defined by the distortions of the past, but by the strength it took to survive them.

In the crucible of validation and self-trust, we emerge as warriors, armed with the knowledge of our own worthiness. We no longer cower in the shadows of manipulation; we stand tall, bathed in the light of our own truth. Through this process, we lay the foundation for healing, reclaiming our narrative, and forging a future free from the shackles of gaslighting and emotional abuse.

Empowering Strategies for Resisting Emotional Manipulation

Armed with the knowledge of emotional abuse and gaslighting, and fortified by the validation of our own experiences, we stand at the threshold of empowerment. This is the realm of resistance, where we forge a path forward, reclaiming our agency and breaking free from the chains of manipulation.

The first pillar of resistance lies in setting and enforcing boundaries. It is a powerful declaration of self-worth, a testament to the belief that we are deserving of respect and consideration. Establishing boundaries requires clarity and conviction. It is an act of self-love, a promise to ourselves that we will not allow our boundaries to be breached. It may be met with resistance, with attempts to push against the edges we have defined. Yet, we stand firm, recognizing that our boundaries are not negotiable.

Communication becomes a vital tool in the arsenal of resistance. It is the bridge that connects us to others, allowing us to assert our needs and assert our truth. Effective communication is rooted in clarity and assertiveness. It is a practice of speaking our truth without apology, of owning our experiences and expressing them with conviction. It may be met with resistance, with attempts to invalidate or dismiss our words. Yet, we continue to speak, knowing that our voice is a beacon of strength.

Self-care emerges as both armor and balm in the journey of resistance. It is the commitment to prioritizing our own well-being, recognizing that we are worthy of the same care and compassion that we extend to others. Self-care is a radical act of self-love, a refusal to sacrifice our own needs for the comfort of others. It may be met with resistance, with accusations of selfishness or demands for our compliance. Yet, we continue to tend to our own well-being, knowing that this act of care is a foundation of our strength.

Building a support network becomes a cornerstone of resistance. It is the recognition that we do not walk this path alone, that there are others who stand with us, who bear witness to our journey. A support network may include trusted friends, family members, or professionals who offer empathy and understanding. It is a refuge in moments of doubt, a source of validation and affirmation. It may be met with resistance, with attempts to isolate us or undermine the credibility of our support system.

Yet, we lean into the strength of our network, knowing that we are not alone.

In the face of resistance, it is important to recognize that we are not simply weathering the storm, but actively shaping the narrative of our own lives. Each act of resistance, each assertion of our truth, is a brushstroke on the canvas of our healing. It is a declaration that we will no longer be held captive by the tactics of manipulation.

As we navigate the terrain of resistance, we do so with a fierce determination. We recognize that our power is not contingent on the approval of others, but on the unwavering belief in our own worthiness. We stand firm in the knowledge that we are not defined by the scars of the past, but by the strength it took to heal them.

In the crucible of empowerment, we emerge as warriors, armed with the tools to resist emotional manipulation. We no longer yield to the whims of manipulation; we stand tall, resolute in our agency. Through this process, we reclaim our narrative, forging a future free from the shackles of gaslighting and emotional abuse.

CHAPTER 5

HEALING FROM NARCISSISTIC ABUSE

Understanding Narcissistic Traits and Behaviors

Navigating the treacherous terrain of healing from narcissistic abuse demands a keen grasp of the traits and behaviors that define this toxic dynamic. It's akin to peeling back the layers of a complex puzzle, revealing the patterns of manipulation and self-absorption that underlie it all.

At the heart of narcissism lies an insatiable hunger for admiration and validation. These individuals exude an aura of grandiosity, masking a profound fragility within. Beneath the veneer of confidence, their self-worth teeters on a precarious edge, easily shattered by even the slightest perceived slight. This paradox is at the core of their being, a delicate dance of dominance and vulnerability.

Empathy, that fundamental cornerstone of human connection, is conspicuously absent in the narcissistic psyche. Their emotional landscape is devoid of the genuine concern and compassion that bind us to one another. Instead, they view relationships through a transactional lens, extracting what they can without regard for the emotional toll it takes on those around them.

Recognizing requires a keen eye, an attunement to the subtle cues that betray the presence of narcissism. The art lies not only in what is said, but in what remains unsaid—the manipulative undercurrents that seek to control and subjugate.

Yet, understanding alone is but the initial step on this arduous journey. It is the lantern that casts light into the darkness, but it does not free us from its clutches. Liberation demands action, a willingness to extricate ourselves from the toxic embrace of a narcissistic relationship.

The tendrils of such relationships run deep, entwining themselves around our sense of self-worth and agency. Breaking free requires a profound act of courage, an unwavering commitment to our own well-being. It's a declaration that we are deserving of respect, of love, of a life free from manipulation and coercion.

As we step onto this path of understanding, we do so with a newfound clarity. We are not defined by the projections and distortions of a narcissistic presence. We are individuals with inherent worth, deserving of healthy, reciprocal relationships.

Armed with this knowledge, we embark on the next phase of our journey: liberation.

Liberating Yourself from a Narcissistic Relationship

The decision to liberate oneself from a narcissistic relationship is a monumental leap towards reclamation. It is a declaration of self-worth, a resounding assertion that we deserve more than the crumbs of conditional love and emotional manipulation.

Breaking free from the clutches of a narcissistic bond is not a linear journey. It's a process fraught with ambivalence, a tug-of-war between the yearning for freedom and the fear of the unknown. The tendrils of manipulation run deep, leaving imprints on our psyche that require tender care and unwavering determination to untangle.

One of the initial hurdles is the recognition that we are not responsible for the narcissist's behavior. It's a revelation that carries both relief and sorrow—a shedding of the heavy cloak of blame we may have unwittingly shouldered. We come to understand that their actions are not a reflection of our worth, but a manifestation of their own internal struggles.

Setting boundaries becomes paramount in this journey to liberation. It's an act of self-preservation, a delineation of our emotional and physical space. This is where we draw the line, where we reclaim the agency that may have been eroded over time. It's a practice that requires practice, a conscious commitment to honoring our own needs and well-being.

In the face of a narcissist's resistance to our newfound boundaries, we are met with a choice: to stand firm in our assertion of self-worth or to capitulate to their demands. It's a crucible moment, one that tests the mettle of our resolve. And as we hold fast to our boundaries, we begin to witness a subtle shift in the dynamic—a reclaiming of power that had long been ceded.

Simultaneously, seeking support becomes a lifeline in this journey. Connecting with others who have traversed similar paths provides validation and a sense of community. It's a reminder that we are not alone, that our experiences are shared by many who have found their way to the other side of healing.

As we inch closer to the precipice of freedom, it's important to acknowledge the grieving process that accompanies the dissolution of a narcissistic relationship. It's a mourning of the hopes and dreams we invested, the illusions we once held dear. This grief is valid, a testament to the depth of our emotional investment.

In the midst of this grief, we begin to catch glimpses of our own resilience. We recognize the strength that has carried us through the darkest moments, the flicker of a light that refuses to be extinguished. It is in these moments that we realize the seeds of our liberation have already been sown, taking root in the fertile soil of our newfound self-worth.

Liberation is not without its challenges, but it is a journey worth undertaking. It is a reclaiming of self, a declaration that we are worthy of love, respect, and genuine connection. As we take each step towards freedom, we do so with the knowledge that we are forging a path towards a future defined by our own agency and inherent worth.

Rebuilding Self-Esteem and Self-Worth

In the aftermath of liberating oneself from a narcissistic relationship, there lies a landscape of emotional wreckage. The foundations of our self-esteem may have been shaken, if not shattered entirely. It is here, in the fertile ground of healing, that we embark on the transformative journey of rebuilding.

Reclaiming our sense of self-worth is a cornerstone of this process. It requires a tender nurturing of the wounded parts within, an affirmation that we are deserving of love, respect, and genuine connection. It's a shift from the narratives of unworthiness that may have taken root during the course of the narcissistic relationship.

Self-compassion becomes a beacon in this journey. It is the gentle hand that guides us through moments of self-doubt and self-blame. It's the reminder that we are not defined by the scars we carry, but by the strength it took to survive and break free. Through self-compassion, we learn to extend the same kindness and understanding to ourselves that we so readily offer to others.

Embracing our authenticity is a powerful antidote to the distortions that may have been imposed upon us. It's a declaration that we are worthy of love and acceptance exactly as we are. This authenticity becomes a source of empowerment, a wellspring from which our self-esteem is replenished.

As we begin to rebuild, we may find solace in creative expression. Art, journaling, movement—these become channels through which we give voice to our experiences and emotions. They are not just mediums of catharsis, but also tools of empowerment, a tangible testament to our resilience.

In this process, cultivating a support network is crucial. Surrounding ourselves with individuals who affirm our worth and celebrate our growth is a balm to the soul. They become mirrors, reflecting back to us the strength and beauty they see within. Through these connections, we anchor ourselves in a community that uplifts and validates.

Self-care becomes an act of devotion to our healing journey. It's a commitment to prioritizing our physical, emotional, and mental well-being. Whether it's a moment of quiet reflection, a walk in nature, or seeking professional support, self-care is the cornerstone upon which our self-esteem is rebuilt.

And in the quiet moments of reflection, we begin to witness the sprouts of our newfound self-worth. It may start as a fragile shoot, but with each act of self-love and self-compassion, it grows stronger, more resilient. We come to understand that our worth was never truly lost; it was merely obscured by the shadows of a narcissistic relationship.

Rebuilding self-esteem is not a linear path, but that of progress and setbacks. It is a testament to our resilience, our capacity to rise from the ashes and redefine our sense of self. As we continue on this journey, we do so with the knowledge that our worth is not contingent on external validation, but an inherent truth that no one can take away.

Thriving Beyond Narcissistic Abuse: Cultivating Healthy Relationships

Emerging from the shadows of narcissistic abuse, we stand at the threshold of a new chapter—one defined by the possibility of genuine, healthy connections. It is a testament to our resilience, a testament to the strength it took to break free from the chains that bound us.

Cultivating healthy relationships begins with a deepening of self-awareness. It's about understanding our own needs, boundaries, and desires. This self-awareness serves as a compass, guiding us towards connections that honor and celebrate our authenticity. It becomes the foundation upon which we build the relationships that will nurture our growth.

Setting boundaries, once a crucial act of self-preservation, now becomes a practice of maintaining healthy connections. It's a declaration of our worth and a safeguard against repeating patterns of toxic dynamics. We communicate our needs with clarity and assertiveness, knowing that in doing so, we create space for relationships to flourish.

Trust, once fractured, is now rebuilt on the solid ground of mutual respect and authenticity. We learn to discern the subtle cues of genuine connection, the steady rhythm of reciprocity and care. It is in this space of trust that we find the freedom to be ourselves, knowing that we are accepted and valued for who we are.

Vulnerability, once a source of pain, is now our greatest strength. It is the bridge that allows us to forge deep connections with others. We learn to share our truths, to let others in, knowing that in our vulnerability, we create space for intimacy and genuine connection to thrive.

As we navigate healthy relationships, self-compassion remains our steadfast companion. It becomes the reminder that we are worthy of love and care, not just from others, but from ourselves as well. Through self-compassion, we continue to tend to the tender parts within, nurturing the seeds of our own growth and well-being.

Communication becomes an art, an art of listening and expressing. We learn to communicate our needs and boundaries with grace and respect. We also learn to truly listen, to hear the needs and desires of others with an open heart. In this exchange, we foster a space where each person's voice is valued and heard.

In the midst of cultivating healthy relationships, we come to realize that our worth is not contingent on the opinions or actions of others. We are inherently valuable, deserving of love, respect, and genuine connection. This knowledge becomes the bedrock upon which we build the relationships that will support and nourish us.

Thriving beyond narcissistic abuse is not just about survival; it is about embracing a life defined by flourishing and growth. It is about stepping into our power, reclaiming our agency, and forging connections that honor and celebrate the beautiful tapestry of who we are. As we continue on this journey, we do so with open hearts and a fierce commitment to living a life rich in healthy, authentic relationships.

CHAPTER 6

THERAPEUTIC APPROACHES TO RECOVERY

Seeking Professional Support: Therapy and Counseling Options

In healing, one of the most vital signposts is professional support. It's the outstretched hand, the guiding voice that can help navigate the complexities of recovery from Complex PTSD. As I stood at this crossroads, I realized that seeking therapy wasn't an admission of weakness, but an assertion of strength.

Therapy, in its many forms, offers a safe space to unearth the buried treasures of our past, to make sense of the fragments of pain and resilience. The process of finding the right therapist can be compated to an interplay of trust and resonance. It requires patience and persistence, a commitment to finding a companion on this journey who understands the nuances of trauma.

The options are diverse, ranging from talk therapy to specialized modalities designed to address specific aspects of trauma. Cognitive Behavioral

Therapy (CBT) unravels the threads of negative thought patterns, offering practical tools to reframe distorted perceptions. Dialectical Behavior Therapy (DBT) equips individuals with skills to regulate emotions and improve relationships.

Person-centered therapy provides a nurturing environment where self-discovery can flourish, while Psychodynamic therapy delves into the depths of the unconscious, illuminating patterns that may have been woven in the shadows. Each approach holds its own unique power, a potential key to unlocking the doors of healing.

Group therapy, too, offers a profound sense of belonging. In the shared stories of others, I found echoes of my own journey, a reminder that I was not alone in this endeavor. It was a sanctuary of understanding, a place where vulnerability was met with compassion, and where the weight of isolation began to lift.

For some, the journey might lead to more specialized forms of therapy. Eye Movement Desensitization and Reprocessing (EMDR) proved to be a revelation in my own path to healing. Through guided bilateral stimulation, EMDR facilitated the reprocessing of traumatic memories, allowing them to be integrated into the narrative of my life in a way that no longer held the power to wound.

The journey of seeking professional support demands a willingness to confront the depths of one's pain, to peel back the layers that have been carefully guarded. It requires vulnerability, a willingness to trust another with the fragments of your soul. But in that vulnerability lies the potential for profound transformation.

It's important to remember that finding the right therapist is a deeply personal process. It's not solely about qualifications and certifications, but about the intangible connection, the sense that this individual is the right guide for your unique journey. Trust your instincts, lean into the resonance you feel, and be patient with yourself as you navigate this crucial step.

As I reflect on my own therapeutic journey, I'm reminded of the courage it took to take that first step, to utter the words that signaled my readiness to confront the ghosts of my past. It was an act of reclaiming agency, a declaration that I was worthy of healing. And in that act, I found a beacon of light amidst the shadows, a promise that I was not alone on this path.

Seeking professional support is a profound act of self-love, a recognition of your inherent worthiness of healing and wholeness. It's a testament to the strength that resides within you, a strength that may have been obscured by the weight of your experiences, but is nonetheless present and resilient. And in the hands of a skilled and compassionate therapist, that strength can be nurtured and amplified, paving the way for a future of possibility and empowerment.

Exploring Healing Methods: EMDR, CBT, and More

For recovery, diverse threads of therapeutic modalities interweave to create a path towards healing. Each method offers its unique insights, a tailored approach to unravelling the complexities of Complex PTSD. Among these, Eye Movement Desensitization and Reprocessing (EMDR) emerges as a transformative force, gently guiding individuals through the process of reintegration.

EMDR, with its foundation in bilateral stimulation, provides a framework for reprocessing traumatic memories. Through a series of guided movements or sounds, individuals engage in a rhythmic flow that taps into the brain's innate capacity for healing. It's as if EMDR holds a mirror to the mind, inviting it to revisit the past with newfound clarity and perspective.

During EMDR sessions, I found myself standing at the intersection of past and present, guided by a skilled therapist who offered both safety and support. Together, we navigated the terrain of my memories, gently untangling the knots that had held me captive for so long. It was a process of discovery, a revelation of the resilience that had always resided within.

Cognitive Behavioral Therapy (CBT) stands as another stalwart in the arsenal of therapeutic approaches. Its focus on the interplay between thoughts, emotions, and behaviors provides a roadmap for reshaping negative patterns. Through the lens of CBT, I learned to identify the distortions that had colored my perception of self and the world.

CBT offered a toolbox of practical strategies, empowering me to challenge and reframe limiting beliefs. It was a process of reclaiming agency, a recognition that I held the power to shape my narrative. As I applied these tools in my daily life, I witnessed a gradual shift in the way I perceived and responded to triggers.

Dialectical Behavior Therapy (DBT) emerged as a beacon of emotional regulation. For those navigating the turbulent waters of Complex PTSD, regulating emotions can feel like traversing a storm. DBT offers a lifeline, equipping individuals with skills to navigate intense feelings while maintaining a sense of groundedness.

Through mindfulness practices, I learned to anchor myself in the present moment, allowing waves of emotion to ebb and flow without being swept away. Distress tolerance skills became a sturdy vessel, providing refuge in the midst of emotional tempests. It was a journey of learning to hold space for my own emotions, to honor them without judgment.

Person-centered therapy provided a gentle embrace, a sanctuary where self-discovery could flourish. Within this empathetic space, I was met with unconditional positive regard, a reminder that my experiences and emotions were valid and worthy of acknowledgment. It was a journey of self-acceptance, a recognition that I was enough, just as I was.

Psychodynamic therapy invited me to descend into the depths of the unconscious, to explore the roots of patterns that had taken hold in the fertile soil of childhood trauma. It was a process of excavation, a willingness to confront the shadows that had shaped my narrative. Through this exploration, I unearthed insights that illuminated the path to healing.

As I immersed myself in these diverse modalities, I realized that there was no one-size-fits-all approach to healing. Instead, it was an intricate dance, a weaving together of methods that resonated with my unique journey. Each modality offered a piece of the puzzle, a key that unlocked a deeper layer of understanding and transformation.

The Role of Mindfulness and Self-Compassion in Recovery

For healing, mindfulness emerges as a golden thread, weaving its way through the fabric of recovery from Complex PTSD. It is a practice that invites us to be present, to anchor ourselves in the here and now, rather than being swept away by the currents of past traumas or anxieties about the future.

Mindfulness, at its core, is a practice of radical acceptance. It invites us to greet each moment with an open heart, to hold space for whatever arises without judgment. Through mindfulness, I learned to witness my thoughts and emotions as passing clouds in the vast sky of my consciousness. It was a powerful shift, a recognition that I was not defined by my experiences, but by the spacious awareness that held them.

Going deeper into mindfulness practices, I discovered the profound impact they had on my nervous system. The gentle rhythm of my breath became an anchor, a lifeline in moments of distress. Through practices like body scans and loving-kindness meditation, I cultivated a sense of safety and presence within my own body.

Self-compassion, too, emerged as a cornerstone of my healing journey. It was a balm for the wounds of self-blame and shame that had lingered for far too long. Through the practice of self-compassion, I learned to extend the same kindness and understanding to myself that I readily offered to others.

Kristin Neff's three components of self-compassion—self-kindness, common humanity, and mindfulness—became guiding principles. I learned to speak to myself with the same tenderness I would offer to a dear friend in times of struggle. I recognized that I was not alone in my pain, that it was a universal human experience. And through mindfulness, I held space for my own suffering without turning away.

Self-compassion became a beacon of light on the darkest days. It was a reminder that I was worthy of love and care, not despite my experiences, but because of them. It was a recognition that my worthiness was not contingent on external validation, but an intrinsic aspect of my being.

The integration of mindfulness and self-compassion became a powerful alchemy. It was a practice of befriending myself, of becoming my own staunch advocate and ally. It was a journey of unlearning the harsh self-critic that had taken residence in my mind, and replacing it with a voice of gentleness and encouragement.

In the stillness of mindfulness, I discovered a sanctuary of self-compassion. It was a space where I could cradle my own wounded heart, where I could offer solace to the parts of myself that had long yearned for validation and tenderness. It was a practice of reclaiming my own worthiness, of recognizing that I was enough, just as I was.

The marriage of mindfulness and self-compassion became a foundation upon which I built my resilience. It was a practice that allowed me to face triggers and flashbacks with a sense of grounded presence. It provided a refuge in moments of overwhelm, a reminder that I could hold myself with the same care that a loving parent holds their child.

As I reflect on this integration, I am reminded that the journey of healing is not linear. It is a dance of progress and setbacks, of moments of clarity and moments of confusion. Yet, through the practice of mindfulness and self-compassion, I have discovered an unwavering anchor, a source of strength that resides within me, ready to support me through whatever challenges may arise.

Integrative Practices for Comprehensive Healing

As I delved deeper into healing from Complex PTSD, I came to understand that true transformation required an integrative approach. It wasn't enough to rely on one modality or practice alone. Instead, it was about weaving together a tapestry of techniques, each complementing and enhancing the others.

At the heart of this integrative approach was the recognition that healing is a holistic endeavor. It encompasses not only the mind, but also the body and spirit. It invites us to tend to our physical well-being, to nourish ourselves with practices that support our overall health.

Physical practices like yoga and somatic experiencing became integral aspects of my healing journey. They offered a bridge between the wisdom of the body and the language of the mind. Through gentle movements and breath awareness, I learned to listen to the signals my body was sending, to honor its innate intelligence.

Yoga, in particular, became a sacred space of embodiment. It was a practice of coming home to myself, of inhabiting my own skin with a sense of presence and reverence. Through asanas and mindful breathwork, I cultivated a deeper connection to my own physicality, a sense of groundedness that provided a sturdy foundation for my healing journey.

Nutrition, too, played a pivotal role in my path to comprehensive healing. I began to view food not only as sustenance, but as a form of self-care. Nourishing my body with wholesome, nutrient-dense foods became an act of love, a way of honoring the vessel that carried me through life's challenges.

In addition to physical practices, creative expression emerges as a powerful tool for integration. Through art, writing, and other forms of creative outlet, we find a language beyond words to communicate and process our experiences. It is a way of giving voice to the unspoken, of externalizing the internal landscape of our healing journey.

Creative expression becomes a sanctuary of catharsis, a space where emotions could flow freely, unburdened by the constraints of language. It is a way of bearing witness to my own journey, of honoring the resilience and creativity that had carried me through even the darkest of times.

The inclusion of body-based therapies, such as massage and acupuncture, provided a somatic anchor in my healing journey. These modalities offered a tangible way to release stored tension and trauma from the body, allowing for a sense of spaciousness and ease. It was a reminder that the body, too, held its own wisdom and capacity for healing.

Nature, with its grounding presence and rhythmic cycles, became a source of solace and inspiration. I found refuge in the embrace of trees, the caress of the wind, and the steady rhythm of the ocean. In the natural world, I discovered a mirror of my own resilience, a reminder that healing is a cyclical process, guided by the seasons of growth and renewal.

The integration of these practices was not without its challenges. It required a willingness to be present with discomfort, to confront the resistance that often arises when we embark on a path of transformation. Yet, in that discomfort, I found the seeds of profound growth, the fertile ground from which true healing could emerge.

CHAPTER 7

PRIORITIZING SELF-CARE AND RESILIENCE

Focusing on Self-Care: Physical, Emotional, and Mental Well-being

Whilst healing, I unearthed a sanctuary nestled within the core of my being. This sacred space became the cradle of my well-being, where I tended to the essential facets of my existence - the physical, the emotional, and the mental.

Physical well-being unfurled as a delicate ballet between movement and repose. I learned to attune to the subtle whispers of my body, responding with grace to its yearnings for gentle stretches or the embrace of a tranquil soak. Nourishment transformed from a perfunctory act to a ritual of self-love. Each morsel I chose bore the intention of nurturing not just my body, but also my spirit. Through food, I rediscovered the profound link between sustenance and self-respect.

Emotional well-being was a canvas on which I painted the hues of self-compassion and vulnerability. I created a sanctuary for my feelings, allowing them to flow without restraint or reproach. Tears, once stifled, now flowed freely as tributaries to the depth of my humanity. In laughter, I found a chorus of resilience, a melody of joy that had always resided within me.

Mental well-being became a garden to tend, a landscape of thoughts that begged for careful cultivation. Mindfulness emerged as my guiding star, beckoning me back to the present whenever the tendrils of anxiety or rumination sought to ensnare me. I embraced the alchemy of affirmations, sowing seeds of positivity that blossomed into a forest of self-assuredness.

As I nurtured my physical, emotional, and mental well-being, a transformation unfolded within me. I sensed the roots of strength weaving through my being, a silent knowing that I was capable of weathering any tempest. The edifice of self-care, painstakingly constructed, became the bedrock upon which my resilience would stand.

In the gentle folds of self-care, I discovered a profound truth: it was not a luxury, but a lifeline. It was the oxygen that invigorated my breath, the sustenance that fueled my odyssey. Through this practice, I unearthed a reservoir of vigor that pulsed through my veins, a testament to the untapped reservoirs of strength within us all.

In the sanctuary of self-care, I found not only healing, but a reclamation of self. It was a gesture of defiance against a world that often demanded more than I could give. It was an act of self-love, a commitment to tenderness, and a promise to honor the vessel that carried me through life's tumultuous seas.

With each deliberate act of self-care, I etched a path towards restoration, a testament to the enduring power of love, both for oneself and for others. It was a revolution born from tenderness, a quiet rebellion that whispered, "I am worthy, I am enough."

In self-care, I discovered the symphony of my own existence, a melody that resonated with the cadence of my heart. And as I moved forward, I carried this newfound wisdom with me, knowing that within the embrace of self-care, I held the key to my own flourishing.

Building Resilience: Strategies for Coping with Triggers and Flashbacks

Resilience, I came to understand, was not a quality reserved for the chosen few. It was a muscle, a skill that could be honed and strengthened through deliberate practice. In the crucible of healing, I forged a resilience that would become my steadfast companion through the ebbs and flows of recovery.

Triggers, those inscrutable messengers from the past, were the crucible in which resilience was tested. They were the echoes of old wounds, the reminders that the journey was not without its shadows. Instead of shying away, I learned to face them head-on, armed with a toolbox of coping strategies.

Breath became my anchor, a steady rhythm that tethered me to the present moment. In the face of a trigger, I would close my eyes and inhale, counting to four, then exhale, releasing the grip of the past. With each breath, I reminded myself that I was here, in this moment, safe and whole.

Grounding techniques became my lifeline. I would run my fingers along the edges of a textured surface, allowing the sensation to pull me back from the precipice of a flashback. I learned to name the objects around me, anchoring myself in the tangible reality of the present.

Journaling became my confidante, a safe space where I could pour out the storm within. Through ink and paper, I gave voice to the turmoil, allowing the words to flow freely, unburdening my soul. It was a catharsis, a release that left me feeling lighter, as if I had cast off a weight I no longer needed to carry.

In the company of supportive friends or a trusted therapist, I found solace. They became witnesses to my journey, offering a steady hand when the path grew treacherous. Together, we unraveled the threads of triggers, dissecting their origins and finding ways to disarm their potency.

Self-compassion emerged as a powerful ally in the face of triggers and flashbacks. Instead of berating myself for feeling vulnerable, I learned to cradle those wounded parts with tenderness. I reminded myself that it was okay to feel, that the echoes of the past were not a reflection of my present strength.

As I practiced these strategies, I witnessed the gradual unfurling of resilience within me. It was a quiet revolution, a testament to the power of intentional healing. I no longer cowered in the face of triggers; instead, I met them with a steady gaze, knowing that I held the keys to my own liberation.

Through building resilience, I discovered a reservoir of strength that ran deeper than I had ever imagined. It was a wellspring of fortitude that had always resided within me, waiting to be tapped. In the crucible of triggers and flashbacks, I forged a resilience that would carry me through the darkest nights.

With each passing day, I felt the tendrils of strength weaving through my being, a quiet assurance that I was capable of weathering any storm. I was no longer defined by my triggers; instead, I was defined by the unwavering resilience that rose to meet them.

Establishing Supportive Connections: Finding Your Community

In healing, I have come to understand the profound importance of community. It was within the embrace of kindred spirits that I found solace, validation, and the unwavering support that became the scaffolding of my recovery.

Finding my community was like discovering a hidden oasis in the desert of isolation. It was a gathering of souls who understood the language of healing, who could look into my eyes and see the echoes of their own journey reflected back. Together, we formed a tribe bound by shared experiences and a collective commitment to growth.

In the presence of this community, I discovered the power of shared vulnerability. It was a space where I could strip away the armor, revealing the raw, unfiltered truth of my journey. Here, I was met with compassion, a reminder that I was not alone in my struggles. In their eyes, I saw the reflection of my own strength, a mirror that affirmed the validity of my experience.

Through shared stories and whispered confidences, I gleaned insights that illuminated my path. I learned new coping strategies, gleaned wisdom from those who had walked similar roads, and discovered the gentle alchemy of collective healing. In this community, I found not only camaraderie, but a wellspring of knowledge and resilience.

Support groups became my sanctuary, a place where I could shed the weight of my burdens and find solace in the understanding nods of fellow travelers. Here, I was met with empathy, a reminder that my pain was not a solitary island, but a thread woven into the fabric of the human experience. Together, we held space for one another, offering a lifeline in moments of despair.

Online forums and social media groups became extensions of this sacred space. They were virtual hearths where I could seek solace at any hour, knowing that a community of kindred spirits was only a click away. Through the digital landscape, I forged connections that transcended geography, finding solace in the knowledge that support knew no bounds.

In the company of my community, I discovered the profound impact of collective healing. It was a symphony of strength, a chorus of voices rising in unison. Together, we shattered the silence that had shrouded our pain, replacing it with a resounding declaration of resilience.

Through shared experiences, I found my own narrative validated and affirmed. I was no longer a solitary traveler; I was part of a greater whole, a testament to the indomitable spirit of the human heart. In the embrace of my community, I discovered a sanctuary that would stand as a pillar of strength through every chapter of my journey.

Tapping into Your Inner Strength: Empowerment and Growth

I unearthed a wellspring of inner strength that had always resided within me. It was a reservoir of power, a quiet force that pulsed through my veins, waiting to be harnessed. As I delved deeper into my journey, I discovered that empowerment was not an external gift bestowed upon me, but an inherent birthright that I could nurture and cultivate.

Empowerment was a dance with self-trust, a recognition that I held the compass to my own healing. It meant honoring my intuition, listening to the whispers of my inner wisdom, and allowing it to guide my steps. Through this practice, I learned to reclaim agency over my own narrative, no longer defined by the expectations or judgments of others.

Setting boundaries like I said became an act of self-preservation, a declaration of my worthiness. It was a practice in honoring my own needs, a reminder that my well-being was not negotiable. I learned to say no without guilt, to protect my energy, and to create a sanctuary of safety within the boundaries I set.

Self-compassion emerged as a beacon of light in moments of darkness. It was a gentle touch on the wounded parts of my soul, a reminder that I deserved the same tenderness and care that I so readily offered to others. Through self-compassion, I learned to be a sanctuary for myself, a wellspring of solace in the midst of life's storms.

Embracing my own growth became a pilgrimage of self-discovery. I no longer shied away from the evolution that was inherent to my being. Instead, I welcomed it with open arms, recognizing that growth was not a betrayal of who I was, but a celebration of who I could become. Through this lens, I learned to view challenges as opportunities for expansion, and setbacks as stepping stones towards greater heights.

In the cocoon of empowerment, I shed the limitations that had bound me. I unfurled my wings, allowing the winds of change to carry me towards new horizons. I no longer feared the unknown; instead, I embraced it as the crucible of transformation.

Through empowerment and growth, I discovered a wellspring of strength that ran deeper than I had ever imagined. It was a quiet force that pulsed within me, a testament to the reservoirs of power that reside within us all. In the crucible of my own healing, I learned that true empowerment was not about seeking power over others, but about harnessing the innate power within myself.

CHAPTER 8

EMBRACING CHANGE AND THRIVING BEYOND TRAUMA

Embracing the Healing Journey: A Lifelong Process

The journey towards healing from complex trauma is not a sprint; it's a marathon. It requires a steadfast commitment to oneself, a promise to navigate the twists and turns, the peaks and valleys, with unwavering determination. There are no shortcuts, no easy fixes. It's a lifelong process that demands patience, self-compassion, and an understanding that healing is not a destination, but a continuous evolution.

As I ventured deeper into this odyssey of self-discovery, I learned to relinquish the need for quick fixes and instant gratification. I embraced the idea that healing is a nonlinear path, where progress is measured not in leaps, but in subtle shifts, in the quiet victories that unfold over time. It was a paradigm shift, a recalibration of my expectations, and it opened the door to a newfound sense of freedom.

The first step in this lifelong journey was to cultivate a relationship with myself built on trust and self-acceptance. It meant facing the mirror, not with criticism, but with a gentle acknowledgment of the strength that resided within. It meant learning to hold my own hand through the storms, to be my own steady anchor in the midst of chaos.

Through therapy and introspection, I began to unearth the layers of conditioning, the beliefs that had taken root in the soil of my psyche. With each revelation came a choice - to cling to the familiar, or to embrace the discomfort of growth. I chose the latter, recognizing that true healing often resides just beyond the edge of our comfort zones.

In this process, I discovered the power of self-compassion, a balm for the wounds of self-doubt and self-criticism. It was a gentle reminder that I was not alone in this journey, that the voice of kindness could drown out the echoes of inner turmoil. Self-compassion became a lifeline, a way to soothe the wounded parts of myself with the same tenderness I would offer to a dear friend.

As the years passed, I witnessed the ebb and flow of healing, the gradual unfurling of petals that had long been tightly bound. There were moments of triumph, where I stood atop metaphorical mountains, surveying the distance I had traveled. There were also moments of quiet introspection, where the seeds of growth were planted in the fertile soil of my soul.

Through it all, I held onto the understanding that healing was not a solitary endeavor. It was a tapestry woven with threads of connection, with the support of those who walked alongside me. The bonds forged in the crucible of shared experience were lifelines, reminders that I was never truly alone in this journey.

And so, as I stand here today, I carry with me the wisdom of a lifetime of healing. I am not defined by the scars of my past, but by the strength it took to heal them. The healing journey, I've come to realize, is not a destination, but a way of being. It is an ongoing commitment to honor the self, to nurture the spirit, and to embrace the ever-unfolding tapestry of life.

Acknowledging Milestones: Recognizing Progress

Milestones are the markers that remind us of how far we've come in healing. They are the signposts along the winding path, offering assurance that progress is not only possible, but tangible. Acknowledging these milestones became a practice that illuminated the subtle shifts and profound transformations that were taking place within me.

The first milestone was a simple yet profound realization - the moment I recognized that I was not defined by my past, but shaped by my ability to transcend it. It was a revelation that infused me with a newfound sense of agency, a belief that I held the power to rewrite my narrative. In that moment, the shackles of victimhood began to loosen, replaced by the steady stride of a survivor.

As I delved deeper into therapy, each session became a crucible of self-discovery, a space where I unraveled the layers of conditioning and unearthed the truths that had long been buried. With each revelation, I celebrated not only the insight itself, but the courage it took to face it. These were milestones of vulnerability, of willingly stepping into the shadows to retrieve pieces of my authentic self.

The journey towards healing also revealed itself in the subtleties of everyday life. It was in the mornings when I woke with a sense of purpose, in the evenings when I laid my head to rest without the weight of unresolved turmoil. It was in the moments of laughter that bubbled up from a place of genuine joy, unburdened by the echoes of past pain. These were the quiet victories, the milestones that whispered, "You are moving forward."

The process of setting and achieving specific goals became a cornerstone of my healing journey. Each goal, no matter how small, became a testament to my resilience and determination. Whether it was learning to establish boundaries, nurturing self-care practices, or daring to dream of a brighter future, each achievement was a testament to my ability to shape my own destiny.

Yet, amidst the celebration of milestones, I learned to hold space for moments of regression and pause. It was important to recognize that healing was not a linear trajectory, but a dance of progress and retreat. These moments were not a sign of failure, but a reminder that growth often occurs in cycles, like the seasons that shift and change.

Acknowledging milestones became a practice of radical self-love, a way to honor the journey I had undertaken. It was a reminder that every step, no matter how small, was a triumph over the shadows of the past. It was a testament to my own resilience, a declaration that I was not only surviving, but thriving in the face of adversity.

As I reflect on these milestones, I am reminded that the healing journey is not defined by its destination, but by the infinite possibilities that unfold along the way. Each milestone is a testament to the strength that resides within, a beacon of light that guides me forward. And so, I continue to walk this path, with gratitude for every step that has brought me to where I stand today.

Cultivating a Purposeful and Gratifying Life

As the tendrils of healing continued to weave their way through my life, I found myself standing at a crossroads. It was a moment of reckoning, a realization that healing was not only about addressing wounds, but about embracing the possibility of a life infused with purpose and gratification.

Cultivating a purposeful life meant daring to dream beyond the boundaries that trauma had imposed. It meant allowing myself to envision a future that was not defined by the limitations of my past. It was a radical act of self-liberation, an assertion that I was worthy of a life that resonated with authenticity and meaning.

The first step in this process was to unearth my passions, to reconnect with the activities and pursuits that brought me joy and a sense of fulfillment. It meant rekindling the flames of creativity that had long smoldered within, giving myself permission to explore, to experiment, and to express myself without inhibition. This act of self-discovery was a reclaiming of my own agency, a declaration that I was the author of my own narrative.

Embracing a purposeful life also entailed aligning my actions with my values, a conscious choice to live in accordance with the principles that resonated deeply within me. It meant setting intentions that reflected my authentic self, and making choices that honored those intentions. It was a commitment to live with integrity, to be a beacon of the values I held dear.

In this process, I learned the power of intentionality, of approaching each day with a sense of mindfulness and presence. It meant savoring the small moments, finding beauty in the ordinary, and recognizing that life's richness often lies in the details. It was a practice that invited me to be fully present in my own life, to relish the journey as much as the destination.

Cultivating a purposeful life also involved nourishing my relationships, surrounding myself with individuals who uplifted, inspired, and celebrated my growth. It meant creating a supportive community, a network of souls who walked beside me on this journey. These relationships were not just a source of comfort, but a mirror that reflected back the strength and resilience I had cultivated within.

As I delved deeper into the aspect of purpose and gratification, I discovered that true fulfillment arose not from external achievements, but from an inner sense of alignment and authenticity. It was about living in a way that resonated with the core of my being, about honoring the unique path I had forged.

In this act of purpose, I found a profound sense of gratification that transcended the transient highs of achievement. It was a contentment that emanated from a life lived in congruence with my deepest self. It was a fulfillment that radiated from the knowledge that I was not just surviving, but thriving in a way that honored my inherent worth.

Extending Support to Others on Their Healing Journey

As the tendrils of my own healing journey spread and intertwined with the world around me, I discovered a profound calling - to be a beacon of support for others navigating their own path to healing. It was a natural progression, a ripple effect born from the seeds of resilience that had taken root within me.

Extending support to others became a testament to the transformative power of healing. It was a way to honor the struggles I had faced, to imbue them with purpose and meaning. It was an acknowledgment that my journey was not solely mine, but part of a collective human experience.

The first step in offering support is to create a safe and nurturing space, a sanctuary where others could unburden themselves and be met with empathy and understanding. It means holding space without judgment, without the need to fix or rescue, but with a deep reverence for each individual's unique journey.

Listening became an art form, a practice of bearing witness to the narratives of pain and resilience that unfolded before me. It was a reminder that healing was not about imparting solutions, but about being a compassionate witness to another's journey. Through this act of deep listening, I learned that sometimes the most powerful support is simply the presence of someone who truly sees and hears you.

In offering support, I learned the importance of empowering others to find their own agency, to recognize the strength and wisdom that resided within them. It meant refraining from imposing my own solutions, and instead, guiding them towards their own inner wellspring of resilience. It was a dance of empowerment, a celebration of their innate capacity to heal.

Sharing my own journey of healing became a bridge of connection, a way to dismantle the isolation that often accompanies the experience of trauma. It was a reminder that we are not alone in our struggles, that there is power in vulnerability and in the knowledge that others have walked a similar path. Through this shared vulnerability, I witnessed the seeds of hope take root in the hearts of those I supported.

Extending support also meant recognizing the importance of self-care, of setting boundaries that safeguarded my own well-being. It was a delicate balance, a reminder that offering support did not mean sacrificing my own health and boundaries. It was a practice of discernment, a commitment to honor both my own journey and the journeys of those I supported.

In the act of extending support, I discovered a profound sense of purpose, a fulfillment that resonated deep within my soul. It was a reminder that healing was not just an individual endeavor, but a collective awakening. It was an affirmation that our stories, our struggles, and our triumphs are threads that weave us together in a tapestry of shared humanity.

And so, I continue to walk this path of extending support, with a heart open to the stories of others, and a deep reverence for the resilience that resides within each of us. It is a privilege and an honor to be a companion on this journey, to bear witness to

the remarkable capacity of the human spirit to heal,
to grow, and to thrive.

www.ingramcontent.com/pod-product-compliance
Lightning Source LLC
Chambersburg PA
CBHW070819280726
48660CB00016B/2142